SHORT BIKE RIDES
IN CONNECTICUT

Jane Griffith *and* Edwin Mullen

The Globe Pequot Press

Old Chester Road
Chester, Connecticut 06412

All photographs are by Henry Hosley, except:
pages 32, 48, and 64 from the State of
Connecticut Department of Commerce.

Second Edition

Second Printing

Introduction

This little book is for all who wish to savor life more. Riding a bike brings about dramatic change in your perceptions. It slows everything down and puts you back in charge. Ride to work some morning instead of going in your car; the world will not go whizzing by anymore. You will see people's expressions and respond to them, discern the shapes of trees, the styles of houses, and take in the scents of the countryside. These are among the joys you miss traveling in the sealed capsule of your car.

These short rides provide an opportunity to explore Connecticut in a unique and rewarding way: by bicycle on hassle-free, planned tours. The rides are from four to twenty-five miles long and range in difficulty from the flat terrain of Stratford to the hills of Salisbury. They can be ridden in a few hours, but to experience all the pleasures of the ride allow at least a half a day. Don't let age deter you from taking these rides. We are forty and fifty, and children aged ten, eleven, and sixteen have also done the rides and had a good time.

To insure your enjoyment, take some precautions and some good equipment: Your bicycle is a vehicle in the eyes of the law and you must obey traffic laws. Secure your bike against theft by using one of the new bolt-cutter-proof locks. This is a *must!* Take along a few simple tools: A screwdriver, pliers, and an adjustable wrench. Take a rag in case your chain really "derails." For picnicking and swimming, pannier bags on your rear rack and handlebar bags are indispensable. You'll need a plastic water bottle, a horn and a headlamp, and a small first aid kit, just in case. As to the bike itself, we recommend a good ten speed model—the best you can afford. A three speed would be all right for the flat country rides but would take the enjoyment out of the others—and that's what it's all about. See you on the road.

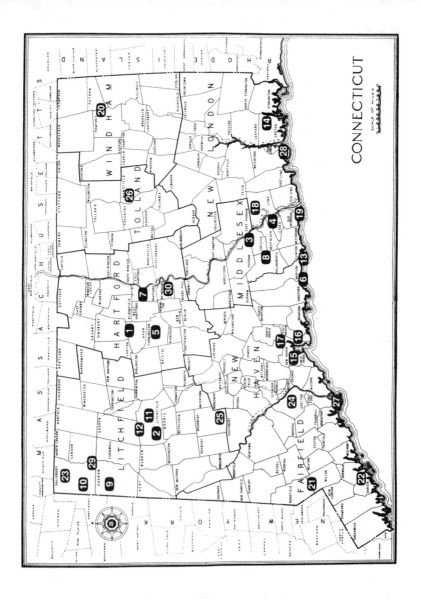

CONNECTICUT

SCALE OF MILES

Table of Contents

Safety

Riding the roads of Connecticut on a bicycle can be dangerous—if you are careless with your equipment or with yourself. Check your bike before you leave. No matter how long
you've been riding use a check list before each ride. The
one that we have used is printed here. Make sure that all
nuts are tight and that the derailleurs and brakes are work-
ing properly. Stay close to the right and observe all of the
traffic laws. You may be caught out after dark so be sure you
have a white light in front and a big reflector in the rear.
Bright clothing also helps.

Check List

1. Brakes
2. Derailleurs
3. Wheel nuts
4. Tires
5. Bolt-cutter-proof lock
6. Tool kit
7. Rag
8. Water bottle
9. Front and rear bags
10. Half roll of toilet paper
11. First aid kit
12. Insect repellent
13. Sunglasses
14. Head protection
15. Wash-N-Dry towelettes
16. Ground cloth
    (for picnicking)
17. Food and drink
18. Towel and bathing suit
19. Money
20. *Short Bike Rides In Connecticut*

1. Avon—Simsbury

Number of miles: 20
Approximate pedalling time: 2 hours
Terrain: mostly gentle, one notably long hill
Surface: fair
Things to see: Avon, Avon Park, Avon Old Farms School, Simsbury, Massacoh Plantation, Ethel Walker School, Stratton Brook State Park

Start from the parking lot at the Old Avon Village Shopping Center. Turn left onto Rte. 44 and immediately left again onto Old Farms Rd. In about two miles you'll arrive at the entrance to Avon Old Farms School which is marked by an enormous brick tower. Turn into the driveway and ride up to the main building. This boys' school is built in the style of an Elizabethan village. It is an enchanting sight. Leave by the exit driveway, turn right at the gate and ride the few yards to Scoville Rd. Turn left onto Scoville; in a half mile turn right onto Burnham Rd. When Burnham "Ts" into West Avon Rd. (Rte. 167), turn right.

Cross Rte. 44 and head toward Simsbury on Rte. 167 (now called Bushy Hill Rd.). There is a long incline on this stretch. After you pass the Ethel Walker School, cross Stratton Brook Rd. at the traffic light and, in about a mile, watch for a BIKE XSSING sign on the right-hand side of the road. This marks the entrance to the bike trail into Stratton Brook State Park. Turn left and head down the trail which takes you through a mile of forest. The trail of hard-packed earth ends at the lake in the center of the park. Here you may swim, hike and picnic.

Return to Rte. 167 on the bike trail. Rte. 167 turns right

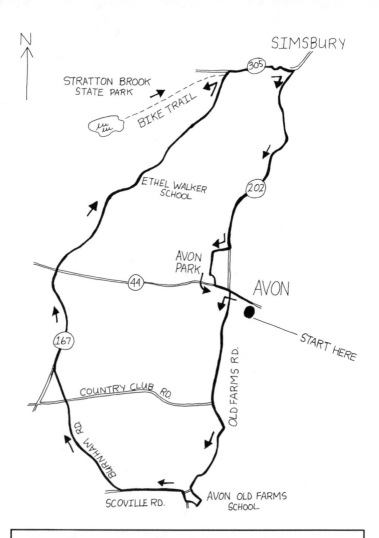

How to get there: from Hartford take Rte. 84 west to Rte. 44, take 44 to Avon; from the west take Rte. 84 east to Rte. 10; take Rte. 10 north to Avon

immediately as it joins Rte. 309 going to Simsbury. At the stoplight marking the intersection of Rtes. 309 and 202 you have a choice: turn right and head toward Avon, four miles away, or take a left and detour through the town of Simsbury and the Massacoh Plantation, an interesting museum on Simsbury's main street. After returning to the intersection of Rtes. 309 and 202, proceed south on 202. A sidewalk along this stretch of highway should be used as the road is narrow and heavily travelled.

Back in Avon, turn right at the Avon Park Theaters' sign. Ride past the theater, following the signs for Avon Park and the Farmington Arts Center. There are exhibits in the Gallery of the Arts Center and artists' studios in the adjoining brownstones. (This delightful complex used to be a fuse factory!) Go out the park's exit to Rte. 44, turn left and return to the Old Avon Village Shopping Center a block and a half away.

2. Bantam Lake

Number of miles: 14
Approximate pedalling time: 1½ hours
Terrain: quite hilly on the east side of the lake, otherwise undemanding
Surface: good
Things to see: Point Folly Camp Ground, Bantam Lake, Litchfield Nature Center, Sandy Beach

The ride begins in Litchfield. Park anywhere along the small Green. Mount up and head west on Rte. 202. In approximately 2¼ miles you will come to North Shore Rd., on the left, across from the sign, "Wamogo Regional High School"; turn left onto North Shore Rd. to start your loop around Bantam Lake, the largest natural lake in Connecticut. In about a mile you will come to Point Folly Camp Ground which is a part of the White Memorial Foundation, a 4,000 acre preserve open to the public. (Near the end of the ride you can visit the Nature Center and Museum.)

North Shore Rd. skirts the end of the lake, winding through an area of modest cottages, swinging to the right, and up a steep, short hill to Rte. 209. Turn left and in about a mile notice Deer Isle, a peninsula. You will pass several restaurants and places to rent boats. About four miles into the ride you'll arrive at the lake's southern end. Start uphill. At the junction of Rtes. 209 and 109, turn left and continue uphill. Just after reaching the crest of the hill you'll spot East Shore Rd. on the left; turn here. At the top of your next climb the road levels off and you'll want to stop to take in the view of the lake. Continue along East Shore Rd. to Sandy Beach which is open to the public. Next continue

13

How to get there: from the south take Rte. 8 to Rte. 118, take 118 to Litchfield; from the west, take Rte. 7 north to Rte. 202, take 202 to Litchfield

about a mile to where East Shore Rd. "Ts" into Alain White Rd.; turn left. Approximately nine miles into the ride turn left onto Bissell Rd. After about one mile turn left into the grounds of the Litchfield Nature Center and Museum. The entrance road is hard-packed dirt. In a half mile you'll arrive at the headquarters of the foundation. Here you'll find a large outdoor map of the center's twenty-five miles of trails. After your ramble through the center, return to Bissell Rd. Turn left then immediately right onto Rte. 202 and head back to Litchfield.

3. Chester—East Haddam

Number of miles: 14
Approximate pedalling time: 2 hours
Terrain: fairly flat on the west side of the river, definitely hilly on the east side
Surface: Good
Things to see: the Connecticut River, Gillette Castle, Goodspeed Opera House, Gelston House Restaurant, towns of Chester and East Haddam

There are many plusses on this ride: the five minute ferry trip on the Chester—Hadlyme ferry, the Rhine River-like view from the terrace at Gillette Castle, the Victorian mood of the Goodspeed Opera House, the varied terrain and, above all, the lively Connecticut River.

Park your car in Chester Center near the handsome stone building which stands at the principal intersection. (The building, incidentally, is NOT a courthouse; it is a package store!) Start by heading east on Rte. 148, crossing Rte. 9A to the Hadlyme Ferry. The ferry operates from April 1 to November 30 from 7:00 A.M. to 8:45 P.M. Bikes only cost a quarter and don't have to wait in line. After crossing the river, proceed up the steep hill to the left for about a mile to Gillette Castle State Park. Be careful on this heavily travelled, narrow road. The Castle, home of a wealthy actor in a bygone era, is a half mile from the park's entrance.

Upon leaving the park turn left. You will now have a very hilly ride to the intersection with Rte. 82, where you turn left. Continue bearing left on Rte. 82. In a little over a mile there will be a stop sign; turn sharply left (still on 82) and you will be exhilarated by the downhill into the town of

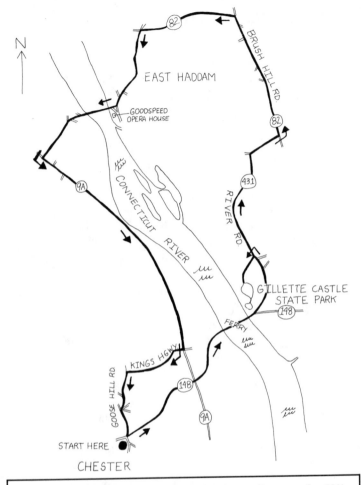

How to get there: from the south, east and west take I95 to the junction with Rte. 9, take Rte. 9 to Exit 6, turn right onto Rte. 148 to Chester; from the north take I95 to the Rte. 9 exit for Middletown, then follow Rte. 9 south to Exit 6 and take Rte. 148 to Chester

East Haddam. While here be sure to visit the Goodspeed Opera House, lovingly and authentically restored in the 1960s, the attractive shops, and the Gelston House Restaurant with its Beer Garden (beer and steamer clams here on a summer day are irresistible). Behind the Gelston House at the riverside you can picnic, watch small airplanes landing on the strip nearby, or the passengers boarding cruise ships for outings on the river and to Long Island. (In the last half of the 1800s steamboat traffic from New York to Hartford brought many fashionable people to the town.)

Upon leaving East Haddam, take the bridge over the river, riding on the solid area close to the railing. Turn left on Rte 9A. In three miles turn right onto King's Highway. Go uphill to the intersection with Goose Hill Rd. Turn left. In about a half mile bear left again, continuing on Goose Hill Rd. which will take you downhill into Chester at the intersection where you left your car.

4. Essex

Number of miles: 13½
Approximate pedalling time: 2 hours
Terrain: gentle to downright hilly
Surface: good
Things to see: Griswold Inn, the Connecticut River, several
marinas, the Copper Beech Inn, Ivoryton Playhouse, and
the Valley RR.

Begin by parking your car behind the Town Hall, just past
the Rte. 9 overpass on Rte. 153 (West Ave.). Mount up and
proceed downhill into Essex proper, passing the Pratt
House and Smithy; bear around to the left following the sign
into Old Essex. Turn right at Main St., and follow it, past the
Griswold Inn, down to the river's edge. Here, at the town
dock, you can take a one hour cruise up or down the
beautiful Connecticut River. Turn around and come up
Main to Ferry St.; turn right. Ferry St. ends at the ferry slip
(for a tiny ferry with a fringe on top to the Essex Island
Marina). After a look at all the dream boats, turn left on
Pratt St., uphill to N. Main St., turn right and within a half
mile you'll find a cemetery on your right. Go into the
cemetery, down to the water's edge. A beautiful spot to rest.
Return to N. Main St. and turn right. Within two miles N.
Main becomes River Rd. After another two miles you'll
come to a stop sign at the juncture of River Rd. and Book
Hill Rd. Make the 160 degree turn left onto Book Hill Rd.
It's a steep hill but after a mile the road goes as steeply
downhill for a fine, free ride for a half mile, until the "T"
intersection of Book Hill and River Rds. Turn right onto
River Rd. and ride a quarter mile to the intersection of

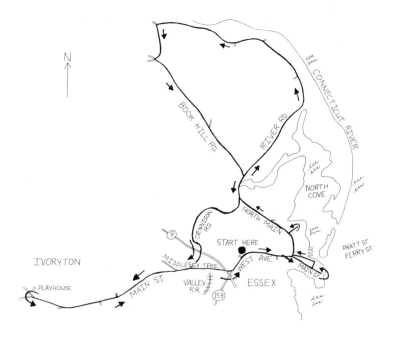

How to get there: from the north, take Rte. 9. south to Exit 3, follow the signs on Rte. 153 into Essex. From the east, take I95 west to Exit 69 to Rte. 9 to Exit 3 and on into Essex. From the west, take I95 to Exit 65. Turn left onto Rte. 153 and follow it to Essex

Dennison Rd. Turn 45 degrees right onto Dennison and you are on the road to Ivorytown, about three miles from this point.

Dennison takes you over Rte. 9 and then to the little town of Centerbrook. At the intersection of Dennison and Middlesex Turnpike, turn right and follow the signs to Ivoryton. Middlesex Turnpike will soon bear almost 90 degrees right. Continue straight on what is now Main St., past the renowned Copper Beech Inn, into Ivoryton.

Check out the Ivoryton Playhouse and the tiny square, then double back on Main St., passing Dennison Rd., bearing right on Middlesex Turnpike, to the Valley Railroad, which is well worth a stop! Continue on Middlesex Turnpike, downhill, under Rte. 9, and immediately left at the traffic light onto West Ave. and you are back in Essex, a third of a mile from the Town Hall and your starting place.

5. Farmington

Number of miles: 14½
Approximate pedalling time: 2 hours
Terrain: varied, some short steep hills
Surface: good
Things to see: Batterson Park, Stanley-Whitman House, Miss
Porter's School, Hill-Stead Museum, the Grist Mill

Leave your car at Batterson Park where you can picnic and swim before or after your ride. Take Batterson Park Rd. about a mile back to the intersection with Fieneman Rd. (the first traffic light). Turn right on Fieneman. Within a half mile you'll come to the intersection of Fieneman, Colt Highway and Birdseye. Continue straight across onto what has now become Mountain Rd. After a mile turn left onto Reservoir Rd., keeping a sharp eye out for traffic coming up Mountain Rd. from your right. In about a mile turn right onto Colt Highway. As you go down this hill, bear diagonally left, following the signs to Rte. 10 at the bottom of the hill. Turn right on 10. Within a mile you'll be in the beautiful town of Farmington. Take a side trip to the Grist Mill by turning left on Mill Lane and going down to the Farmington River. Back on Main St. (Rte. 10), ride by the Congregational church and the buildings of Miss Porter's School. Cross Farmington Ave., go about two miles and turn right on Aqueduct Lane. After climbing this very steep hill to Talcott Notch Rd., turn right. At Mountain Spring Rd. turn right again and within another mile and a half you'll be back at Farmington Ave. Turn right onto Farmington, go down a short, steep hill to High St. where you turn left.

Midway up High St. you'll see the Stanley-Whitman House (1660). It's open to the public except on Mondays.

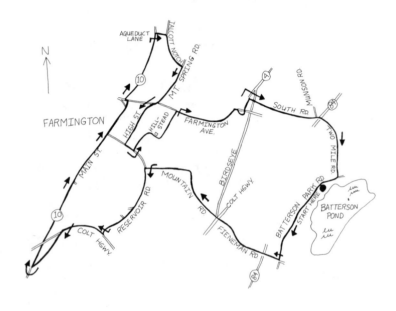

How to get there: from the north, take Rte. 84 to Exit 37 (Fieneman Rd.), follow the signs to Batterson Park; from the south take I91 to Exit 21, then Rte. 72 west to Rte. 84, then take 84 to Exit 37 and to Batterson Park

There is a small entrance fee. When you reach Mountain Rd. turn left and go a short distance uphill to the entrance driveway to the Hill-Stead Museum. Turn left and ride through the grounds of the Stanford White-designed house. Hill-Stead, with its collection of impressionist paintings and elegant furniture and appointments, is open on Wed., Thurs., Sat., and Sun., from 2 to 5 P.M. A moderate admission fee is charged. Continue on the driveway around the back of the house and through the property. You will come back out on Farmington Ave. (Rte. 4). Turn right. In a half mile, follow Rte. 4 east as it circles 90 degrees left, crossing Farmington Ave., then turn right onto South Rd. In a mile, Munson Rd. will merge into South Rd. from the left. Go over the highway and continue for about a half mile on what is now called Two Mile Rd. to Batterson Park.

6. Guilford

Number of miles: 20½
Approximate pedalling time: 2½ hours
Terrain: mostly gentle, a couple of tough hills
Surface: good
Things to see: Guilford Green and Marina, Henry Whitfield
House, Hyland House, Griswold House, Monastery of Our
Lady of Grace

This ride originates in North Guilford at the junction of Rtes. 80 and 77 where you may park. Ride south on Rte. 77. The road declines gently toward Guilford and the sea. After about five and a half miles you'll come to the Guilford Green. This is one of the loveliest Commons in New England. It is flanked by a spired white Congregational church, stately houses and quaint shops. At the Green turn right onto Broad St. and then left on Whitfield St. which will take you down to the Sound. In a mile you will see the striking Henry Whitfield House on the left. Built in 1639 with dense stone walls, a 60 degree sloping tiled roof, leaded windows and twin chimneys, it is reputedly the oldest stone house in America. It is furnished with period pieces and is open to the public. Visit it if you have time and then ride over the railroad tracks for a sweeping view of the Sound and the reed-rich marshes characteristic of the Connecticut shoreline. Proceed to the marina past the Beecher House (1740). At the marina there are three good restaurants to tempt you, or you can have a picnic sitting on the rocks at harborside.

On the return, ride up Whitfield taking Old Whitfield for a short distance to bring you to the Henry Whitfield

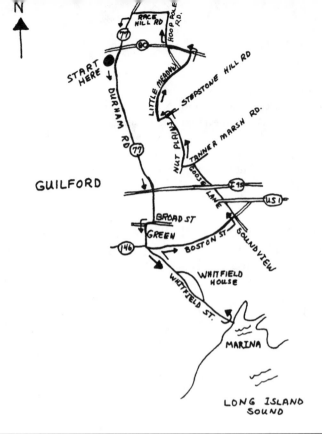

N

START HERE

GUILFORD

RACE HILL RD.
HOOP POLE RD.
LITTLE MEADOW
STEPSTONE HILL RD
DURHAM RD
77
77
80
NUT PLAINS
TANNER MARSH RD.
GOOSE LANE
I-95
US1
BROAD ST
GREEN
146
BOSTON ST
SOUNDVIEW
WHITFIELD HOUSE
WHITFIELD ST.
MARINA

LONG ISLAND SOUND

How to get there: from the north, take I91 to Exit 8 (Rte. 80). Take 80 east to the junction with Rte. 77. From the west, take I95 to Exit 55. Turn right at the bottom of the ramp onto US1 and go a short distance to the junction with Rte. 139. Turn left onto 139 and go about two miles to Rte. 80. Turn right (east) onto 80 and go four miles to the junction of 80 and 77. From the east take I95 to Exit 61, go north on Rte. 79 to 80, then go west on 80 to 77

House. Old Whitfield brings you back to Whitfield St. Proceed back to the Green. Turn right at the foot of the Green onto Boston St. (it may not be marked). Notice the Hyland House (1660) and the Griswold House (1735) both open to the public. Ride to Soundview Rd. You are now approximately nine miles from your starting point. Turn left, going under the turnpike. Soundview becomes Goose Lane. In about a mile, Goose Lane turns left where Tanner Marsh Rd. comes in from the right. Continue on Goose Lane for about one half mile to where Nut Plains Rd. comes in from the left. There is an old, small cemetery on the right; keep to the right. Goose Lane is now Nut Plains Rd. which soon "Ts" with Stepstone Hill Rd. (to the right this road is called No. Madison Rd.). Go left up very steep Stepstone Hill Rd. and turn right near the top of the hill onto Little Meadow Rd. Now you'll have a downhill swing on Little Meadow Rd. all the way to Rte. 80. (Bear right at the fork formed by Little Meadow and Hoop Pole Rds.) When you reach Rte. 80, turn left and go uphill about seven-tenths of a mile to Hoop Pole Rd. Turn right. After going uphill past ponds and woods you'll come to Our Lady of Grace Monastery (Dominican nuns). Turn left here onto Race Hill Rd. Savor the Grandma Moses scene off to the right after passing the monastery. Turn left at the bottom of the hill onto Rte. 77 (Durham Rd.) and return to your car at the junction with Rte. 80.

7. Hartford

Number of miles: 11
Approximate pedalling time: 1½ hours
Terrain: generally rolling; three hills
Surface: fair to good; watch for roadwork in progress
Places to see: Constitution Plaza, Old State House,
    Wadsworth Atheneum, Bushnell Plaza and Park, State
    Capitol, State Museum, Mark Twain House, Harriet
    Beecher Stowe House, Elizabeth Park, Governor's
    Mansion, Hartford Civic Center

Park your car near award-winning Constitution Plaza on Columbus Blvd. Start your ride on State St. in front of Broadcast House. Turn left onto Prospect St. passing in front of the Old State House on Thomas Hooker Square. Go two blocks to Atheneum Square North; turn right. You will pass the Traveler's Insurance Co., the Avery Memorial and the Wadsworth Atheneum, a nationally recognized fine arts museum. Cross Main St. passing Bushnell Plaza. Go downhill to Bushnell Park. Ride into the park and cross it on the diagonal crossway. You will come out of the park at the corner of Elm and Trinity Sts.; turn left. The stone arch on the right is a Civil War memorial.

At the top of the hill turn right and circle around the Capitol, passing the State Museum on the left. You can see the Armory below the Capitol as you make the circle. When you come around to the side of the Capitol overlooking the city, take the paved pathway going down the hill, bearing left on the intersecting path to Asylum St. Turn left on Asylum and when Asylum forks, bear left on Farmington.

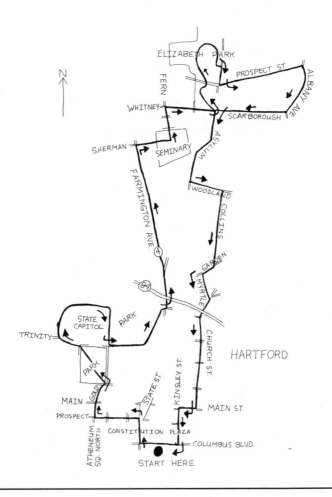

How to get there: take the State St. Exit 31 from I91 if you are coming from the north or south, or the State St. Exit from Routes 84 or 15 if you are coming from east or west

On this street you will pass some of the insurance companies, for which Hartford is famous, and the new cathedral.

After three miles on Farmington you will come to Nook Farm. On this tract stand the houses of two of America's most celebrated writers, Mark Twain and Harriet Beecher Stowe. The houses are open to the public. Turn right onto Sherman St. which curves left in the middle of the Hartford Seminary and becomes Fern St. Go up Fern to Whitney. Turn right onto Whitney and then left into Elizabeth Park at the corner of Whitney and Asylum. Circle through the lower half of the park, then cross Prospect and enter the upper half of the park. Ride around the superb Rose Garden back to Asylum Ave.; turn right. At the corner of Prospect and Asylum, where the Governor's Mansion is located, turn left. A long hill leads you past the mansion to Albany St. Turn right, ride downhill to Scarborough St. Turn right onto Scarborough and go to Asylum and turn left.

Proceed to Woodland St.; turn left here (at the St. Francis Hospital and Medical Center), then turn right on Collins St. Ride about seven blocks on Collins then turn right onto Garden St. Go up a short, steep hill and turn left onto Myrtle. Go downhill for one block, bearing right (Myrtle becomes Church St. here), then left under the RR station. You will pass the mammoth Hartford Civic Center. Church St. "Ts" into Main St. in front of the well-known G. Fox and Co. store. Turn left; go a scant block to Talcott St. Turn right onto Talcott and ride down to Columbus Blvd. and your car.

8. Killingworth

Number of miles: 13½
Approximate pedalling time: 2 hours
Terrain: demanding
Surface: good
Things to see: Country Squire Inn and Antique Shop, several
    fine churches and houses, Chatfield Hollow State Park

This ride is a country workout for you and your equipment; we recommend that you not tackle it until you have done a lot of riding (unless you are in good shape anyway).

Start at the intersection of Rtes. 80 and 81. Head east on Rte. 80 toward Winthrop and Deep River. You will pass the well-known Country Squire Inn immediately on the left where you might let yourself be tempted by both the good food and the antiques in the shop adjoining. In about two and a half miles after an uphill and a downhill you'll enter the township of Deep River, passing a lake and Rte. 145 south on your right. A little further up the road, about four miles into the ride, turn left on Rte. 145 north which is little more than a country lane. (The sign to 145 north is practically hidden, but a country church on your left as you reach the crest of the hill marks the spot.)

Moderate up and downhill swings characterize the first part of this stretch on Rte. 145 north. You will ride through a Hobbit-like glen where the tree shaded road snakes right and left; no doubt orks dwell in this part of the forest. After about two and a half miles there is a sign to Chester Airport; if you enjoy watching small planes take off and land, turn right up the brief hill to the field.

The difficult part of the ride comes up when you turn

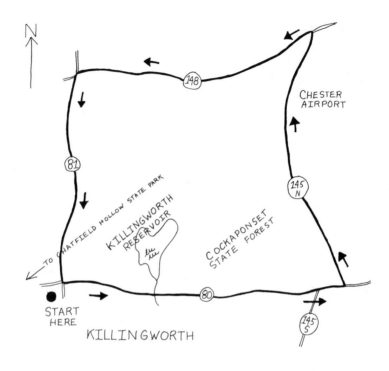

How to get there: from the south, take 195 to Exit 63. Head north on Rte. 81 to Rte. 80; from the north take I91 to Exit 7 to Rte. 80 and proceed to the junction with Rte. 81, or follow Rte. 9 out of Middletown to Rte. 81 then head south on 81 to Rte. 80

left at the intersection of Rtes. 145 and 148. This leg of the ride is a grueling three and a half miles of uphill riding, all the way to Rte. 81. When you reach Rte. 81, turn left and head back to your starting point. Just before you get to the intersection of Rtes. 80 and 81 where you parked your car, take a look at Killingworth's perfect Congregational church on the left.

Before you head home, wrap up the day with a visit to Chatfield Hollow State Park which is only a mile to the west on Rte. 80 from where your car is parked. Bike or drive down the roller coaster hill to the park where you can swim and picnic and enjoy the coolness of the hollow after your workout.

9. Lakeville—Sharon

Number of miles: 14
Approximate pedalling time: 2 hours
Terrain: hilly
Surface: good
Things to see: Salisbury, Lake Wanonscopomuc, Lakeville,
    Hotchkiss School, Mudge Pond, Sharon

Park your car on Main St. in Lakeville. Head west on Rte. 44
which takes you up and down brief hills following the shape
of Lake Wanonscopomuc. At the top of a hill you will come
to a fork; bear left. You are now on Indian Mountain Rd.
Soon you will have a half-mile-long downhill. At the bottom
of it there is a 4-way stop sign where Rte. 112 crosses your
street. When you get to the top of the next ridge, you have a
wonderful view of neighboring valleys and hillsides. Soon
there is a mile-long downhill sweep, then the road levels off,
narrows, and "Ts" almost imperceptibly into Mudge Pond
Rd. The road turns a sharp right and then a sharp left as it
nears the pond. Now the route is flat, skirting the pond
where there are places to picnic and swim.

    The route along the pond is about a mile and a half
long. Then comes a steep uphill which takes you out of the
valley and yields an expansive view of it. Now the road goes
down and "Ts" into Millerton Rd. (Rte. 361). Turn left
toward the town of Sharon. Just before the town, the road
climbs steeply past a cemetery on the left and then it "Ts"
into West Main St. at the Sharon Green. Explore the village
and then turn north on Main St. (Rte. 41). Rte. 41 goes uphill
out of town. From the crest is some of the state's finest
scenery. You are skirting a ridge here going uphill gently at

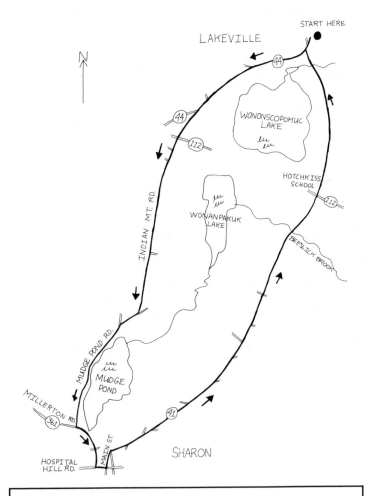

How to get there: from the southwest take Rte. 7 to Cornwall Bridge then follow Rtes. 4, 41 and 44 to Lakeville; from Hartford and the east take Rte. 44 to Lakeville

first and then more steeply for three-tenths of a mile, followed by a half-mile-long downhill. This is followed by a long, gradual incline. At the crest, stop to enjoy the panorama, rare for Connecticut. Another long hill takes you to the junction with Rte. 112. Here ride through the grounds of Hotchkiss School if you like, then continue north on Rte. 41 enjoying the remaining two miles of the ride which are generally downhill.

10. Lake Waramaug

Number of miles: 8
Approximate pedalling time: 1¼ hours
Terrain: flat
Surface: good
Things to see: the lake itself, Boulder Inn, The Inn at Lake
  Waramaug, Hopkins Vineyard Winery, Lake Waramaug
  State Park

Start the ride at the small but lovely Lake Waramaug State
Park. There is ample parking. This park provides camping
areas, swimming and picnic grounds, so after you've cir-
cuited the lake plan to spend some time at the park. Mount
up and proceed to the right, counterclockwise around the
lake. The route is relatively flat and affords fine views of the
lake, a large one set down at the base of surrounding hills
which are covered with magnificient foliage, especially in
the fall.

After four miles of easy riding along the shore of the
lake, you will come to the southern end where there is a
commercial boat launching area, a restaurant and a beer
parlor, as well as a town beach. Next is a short uphill stretch
on Rte. 45, leveling off near the Boulder Inn, which offers
lodging and dining and has a fine view of the lake. In less
than half a mile you'll come to Lake Rd.; turn left, leaving
Rte. 45 and continue your circuit. Lake Rd. is a tiny, narrow
road that twists and turns, following the natural contours of
the shoreline. On this stretch you'll pass the Hopkins Vineyard Winery and The Inn at Lake Waramaug. This fine old
inn, set on a hillside overlooking the lake, has property on
the lake front, where there are sailboats and swimming and
picnicking for the guests.

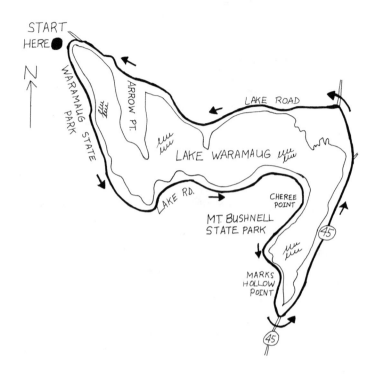

START HERE

N

WARAMAUG STATE PARK

ARROW PT.

LAKE ROAD

LAKE WARAMAUG

LAKE RD.

CHEREE POINT

MT. BUSHNELL STATE PARK

MARKS HOLLOW POINT

45

45

How to get there: from the south take Rte. 47 to Rte. 25 (202), turn left and proceed to Rte. 45, turn right and go to the lake. Drive along the lake on Rte. 45 to Lake Rd. Turn left and proceed to Lake Waramaug State Park; from the northeast take Rte. 44W to Rte. 25 (202) through Torrington and Litchfield to Rte. 45, then proceed as above

As you continue on Lake Rd. you will be struck by the fact that long stretches of the shoreline have not been developed; fields go right down to the water's edge in some places. This is one of the few lakes we have seen which is not entirely taken over by signs saying PRIVATE KEEP OUT, so riding here is particularly unhurried, unharried and joyful. Around the next bend you will be able to see the state park. When you come to the entrance, turn left and you are back at your starting place. We took this ride in October (when the woods were wild with color) and as we rounded the bend into the park we came upon two cyclist-campers who were taking a swim after putting up their tent and making camp; as we loaded our bikes for the trip home, we vowed to come back and camp there the following summer.

11. Litchfield

Number of miles: 4
Approximate pedalling time: 1 hour
Terrain: flat in town, two hills getting in and out
Surface: good
Things to see: Litchfield itself, with its 18th century houses,
the first law school, Litchfield Historical Museum and the
18th century Congregational church

This ride starts at the Litchfield Green. At the intersection
of Rtes. 202 and 63 (South St.), turn right onto South St. Just
around the corner there is an entrance into Cobble Court,
an old cobblestone courtyard bordered with fascinating
shops. Continue down South St. which is flanked on both
sides by 18th century houses. The first law school in America is here; it was started in 1775 by Tapping Reeve whose
brother-in-law, Aaron Burr, was his first pupil. It matriculat-
ed more than one thousand students before it closed in
1833.

When you get to the intersection of South St. and Old
South St., notice the Ethan Allen House, built in 1736; this
house is believed to have been the birthplace of the Revolu-
tionary War hero. Follow Old South Rd. for approximately
1.3 miles as it loops back to South St., where you turn left
and go uphill back to the Green. On South St. the sidewalk is
broad and passes close to the lovely old houses; it's a good
place to ride if there is not too much pedestrian traffic.
Watch for the Oliver Wolcott, Sr. House; Wolcott, governor
of Connecticut, was a signer of the Declaration of Indepen-
dence. Turn right when you arrive at the Green, circle
around the end of the Green and proceed to the intersec-

N

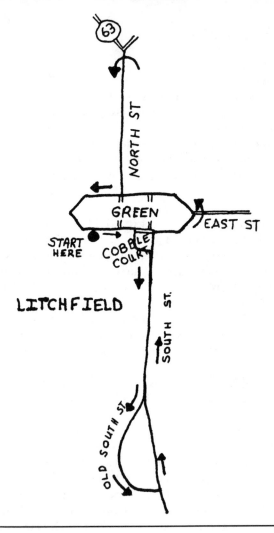

63

NORTH ST

GREEN

EAST ST

START HERE

COBBLE COURT

LITCHFIELD

SOUTH ST.

OLD SOUTH ST.

How to get there: from the south take Rte. 8 to Rte. 118, take 118 to Litchfield; from the west, take Rte. 7 north to Rte. 202, take 202 to Litchfield

tion with North St. (Rte. 63 north) There are stately homes on both sides of North St. including, on the west side, Sheldon's Tavern where George Washington once slept. Go up one side of North St. and down the other, using the Alexander Catlin House (1778), at the "Y," as the turn-around point. Return to the Green.

Before leaving Litchfield proper, try to make time to visit the Litchfield Historical Society located on the corner of South and East Sts. The society, open Tuesday through Saturday from 11 A.M. to 5 P.M., has displays in its four galleries and an outstanding manuscript collection of old Litchfield.

12. Litchfield County

Number of miles: 12
Approximate pedalling time: 2 hours
Terrain: definitely hilly
Surface: mostly good; some bad spots
Things to see: Kilravock Inn, superb Connecticut farmland
and woods, fine houses of Litchfield

This ride starts at the Litchfield Green. Turn left onto Rte.
202 and ride approximately one mile to where Brush Hill
Rd. goes off at a 45 degree angle to your right. Turn right
onto Brush Hill Rd. and in about one-half mile you will pass
a long, low stone wall on the left. This was the site of the
former Kilravock Inn. In the original edition of our book the
Litchfield rides started from this inn. Alas, the beautiful inn
burned to the ground and is no more.

After a mile and a half of uphill riding through the
woods, Brush Hill becomes Maple St. Continue on Maple
when Litwin Rd. intersects with Maple from the left. Soon
you will come to the intersection of Maple with Milton Rd.;
turn right onto Milton which meanders, and goes uphill and
down (as do all these roads). You will pass the challenging
Stony Brook Golf Course. Two miles after turning onto
Milton you will come to Osborn Rd. on your left. Turn up
Osborn for a short, steep push. Within a half mile Osborn
merges with Beach St.

Join Beach St. bearing slightly left. We suggest you
picnic along here. Our lunch under a stately tree was ac-
companied by the lowing of a clutch of mildly curious cows
on the other side of the fence. After you mount up you can
enjoy the views occasionally revealed through the trees and

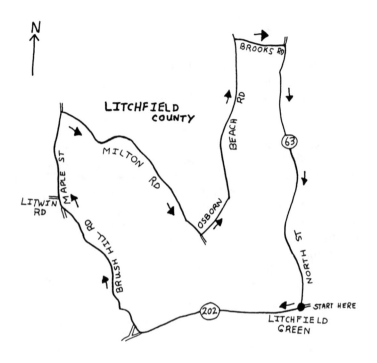

N

LITCHFIELD COUNTY

BROOKS RD

BEACH RD

63

MILTON RD

OSBORN

MAPLE ST

LITWIN RD

BRUSH HILL RD

NORTH ST

START HERE

LITCHFIELD GREEN

202

How to get there: from the south, take Rte. 8 to Rte. 118, take 118 to Litchfield; from the west, take Rte. 7 north to Rte. 202, take 202 to Litchfield

the enormous country places you will pass. Two miles from the intersection of Osborn and Beach you will come to Brooks Rd.; turn right. It immediately goes downhill then abruptly uphill before descending to Rte. 63. Brooks Rd. "Ts" into Rte. 63. There is a stop sign for you; be cautious.

You are about three miles from Litchfield and you face a couple of arduous uphill climbs, barely relieved by brief downhills. In Litchfield, Rte. 63, also called Goshen Rd., becomes North St. This street is flanked by some of America's architectural treasures. The houses here, and on South St. on the opposite side of the Green, have earned Litchfield the designation, Historic District.

13. Madison—Hammonasset

Number of miles: 17
Approximate pedalling time: 2½ hours
Terrain: flat to slightly hilly
Surface: good
Things to see: the shoreline town of Madison with its exceptional Congregational Church, Hammonasset State Park

Start in the parking lot of the Sachem Country House on Goose Lane in Guilford. Turn left, go under the turnpike to the intersection with US1, turn left and go up a short hill. One mile into the ride brings you to the East River. Here there are marshes on both sides of the road and you'll enjoy a lovely view of the Sound. About a half mile from the East River, turn left onto Wildwood Ave. which takes you through the country part of Madison, fine in the summer and even better in the fall. The road snakes around to the right and forks; take the right fork. Soon you pass Nortontown Rd. and your road becomes Greenhill. The Munger Lumber Company suddenly appears, and then another fork; bear right. The road starts uphill at this point, levels off as you pass Copse Rd., and then goes briefly uphill again.

At the four mile point Greenhill crosses Rte. 79. Continue on Greenhill which curves around and down to the intersection with Horsepond Rd. Turn right onto Horsepond which has a wide shoulder. Within a mile and a half Horsepond goes off to the right, continue straight on your present road which becomes Duck Hole Rd. At the intersection of Duck Hole with Rte. 1 there is a traffic light at the bottom of a hill. Cross over and enter Hammonasset State

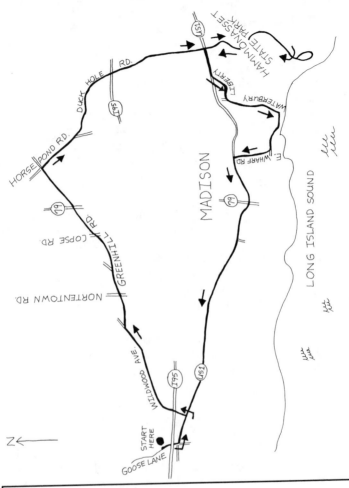

How to get there: from the west take I95 to exit 59, turn left at the end of the ramp and go under the turnpike to the parking lot at the Sachem Country House; from the east take Exit 59 from I95 and turn right to go to the parking lot

Park. There's no charge for bicycles, so lock up and have a swim.

Come back out to Rte. 1 and turn left. The road goes gently up and down and at the bottom of the third hill there is a caution light. Turn left onto Liberty St. At Waterbury Ave. turn left and ride down to the shore for an uncluttered view of the Sound. Turn right at the stop sign at East Wharf Rd. Soon East Wharf "Ts" into Rte. 1. Turn left and go through the brief but well manicured shopping section. After passing the intersection of Rte. 79 and Rte. 1 (Main St.) you will come upon the Green. Bear right and loop around the Green passing in front of the magnificent First Congregational Church, built in 1707. Return to Rte. 1 and continue on it past West Wharf Rd. and the cemetery. Return to Goose Lane in Guilford and the Sachem Country House where you left your car.

14. Mystic—Stonington

Number of miles: 14½
Approximate pedalling time: 2 hours
Terrain: generally flat, three hills
Surface: good to only fair in spots; good shoulders where
    needed
Things to see: Mystic, Mystic Seaport Museum, Stonington,
    Old Stone Lighthouse, Mystic Marinelife Aquarium

Park in the south parking lot of Mystic Seaport Museum, just across from its entrance. Mount up and turn left onto Main St. Turn immediately right on Isham St. Ride the brief block to the Mystic River. Notice the old schooner, the *L.A. Dunton,* on the way. It is in the process of being restored (Nov. 1982). Turn left onto Bay St. When Bay "Ts" into Holmes St., turn right. At the stop sign, turn left on East Main St., then turn right at the Civil War Memorial onto US1. Stonington is four miles away. In about three miles, St. Mary's Cemetery will be on your right. Make a loop through it and turn right, back onto US1. Turn right on US1A (Water St.) toward Stonington Village.

    Turn left on Trumbull Ave. You will soon come to a stop sign at the foot of the only bridge over the RR tracks; turn right over the bridge, then turn left onto Water St. and begin the ride down to Stonington Point. The whole town is rich with 18th century buildings so you'll probably want to explore it thoroughly. Just after Pearl St. there is a tiny restaurant, The Pilot House, where you can enjoy their sweet Portuguese bread or hearty Portuguese soup. Just before the end of Water St. you will see the Old Stone Lighthouse which is open to the public every day except

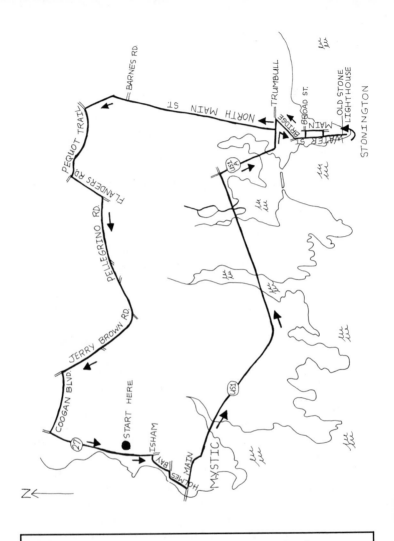

How to get there: from the west and east take the Mystic Exit from I95 onto Rte. 27 and follow the signs to Mystic Seaport

Monday from 11:00–4:30 P.M., May through Oct. for a small fee. At the point you are at the halfway point of the ride.

Proceed back up Water St. until you spot the sign that directs all traffic to the right around a tiny park. Turn right and then left onto Main St. Notice the Old Custom House and the Portuguese Holy Ghost Society, a reminder of the Portuguese fishermen who add zest to the town's culture. Turn left on Broad St. and then right on Water St. to go back over the bridge. On the other side of the bridge, take an immediate left onto Trumbull and then a right onto North Main St. which quickly becomes a country road. Two and a half miles after your turn onto North Main St., you'll come to a "T" intersection with Pequot Trail; turn left. After you see the "Road Church" on your left and just before the road goes over the turnpike, turn left onto Flanders Rd. (it may not be marked). In three-tenths of a mile turn right onto Pelligrino Rd. and go uphill. Continue on Pelligrino when Montauk Ave. comes in from the left. After the stop sign, just past Deans Mill Rd., continue straight. Pelligrino Rd. becomes Jerry Brown Rd. at the point where Mistuxet comes in from the left. Continue on Jerry Brown Rd. uphill and down. Turn left onto Coogan Blvd. just before going under the turnpike. Coogan goes past the Mystic Marinelife Aquarium and the Old Mistick Village Shopping Center. Coogan "Ts" into Rte. 27 at a busy intersection in a snarl of motels and gas stations. Turn left and head back to Mystic Seaport.

15. New Haven—East Rock

Number of miles: 9
Approximate pedalling time: 1¼ hours
Terrain: flat in the city, then up and down fabulous East Rock
Surface: good
Things to see: New Haven Green, New Haven Colony
    Historical Society, Peabody Museum, East Rock Park and
    THE VIEW, Lake Whitney, Edgerton Park

This is a spectacular nine mile circle from the New Haven Green to the summit of East Rock and back. You won't believe you did it until you reach the top of East Rock, 365 feet above the plain, and suddenly see all of the city and surrounding countryside, the harbor, and Long Island Sound below you!

The ride begins at the corner of Elm and Church Sts. at the Green. Head north on Church St. In two blocks you will notice that Church changes its name to Whitney Ave.—it's a fine old New England custom.

At the corner of Sachem and Whitney you'll pass the Peabody Museum of Natural History and other buildings of Yale University. Proceed to Edwards St. Take a right on Edwards and a left onto Livingston. At the corner of Cold Spring St. and Livingston you will find yourself at College Woods, a part of East Rock Park. Proceed to East Rock Rd. Turn right and cross the Mill River. Dead ahead you'll confront 365 feet of stone: the near vertical face of East Rock. Turn left onto Farnum Dr. to begin your gradual climb. Farnum Dr. makes a long loop to the meadow on the north, and then snakes its way to the summit.

The ride down is heavenly! Take the same route, bear-

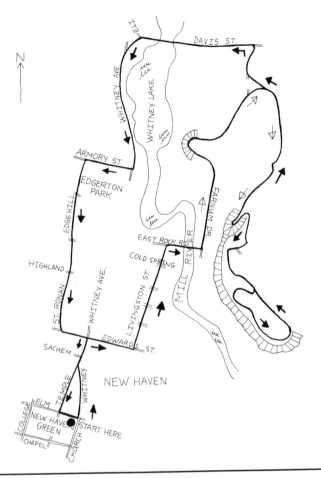

How to get there: from the north take I91 to Exit 3; follow Trumbull to Temple St.; turn left and proceed three blocks to the Green; from the east or west take I95; at New Haven follow the signs to Downtown New Haven. Take the first exit (Church St.) turn right onto Church and proceed to the Green

ing left at the first fork and right at the second. Turn left when Farnum "Ts" into Davis St. Cross the bridge over Lake Whitney, and bear left at the intersection formed by Eli and Davis Sts. Ride a few yards up the hill to the traffic light on Whitney Ave.; turn left.

At the next traffic light turn right onto Armory St. The property on the left which resembles a fortification from Quebec is in fact a storage facility of the New Haven Water Company. The little house on the corner, 1799, was a boarding house for Eli Whitney's gun factory. Go one block to Edgehill Rd. and turn left. At number 145 Edgehill there is a secret garden: Edgerton Park—a walled park of several rolling acres which is open to all. There is also a mystery: where is the mansion of the estate? Alas, it was destroyed at the stipulation of the donors in their will.

Edgehill becomes St. Ronan when you cross Highland. When St. Ronan "Ts" into Edwards St., turn left and go downhill to Whitney where you turn right. Best to take the sidewalk here. Whitney forks at the mini-park at Trumbull St.; bear right. Cross Elm and enjoy New Haven's picturesque Green before returning to your car.

16. New Haven—Lighthouse Point

Number of miles: 13
Approximate pedalling time: 2 hours
Terrain: flat with several small hills
Surface: good to excellent
Things to see: New Haven Green, Morris Cove, Lighthouse
Point Park, the Pardee Morris House, Wooster Square

This ride starts at the New Haven Green, on the corner of
Church and Elm Sts. You can park your car at any spot
around the Green. Go east on Elm over the railroad tracks;
bear right onto Olive St. Continue on Olive about one-half
mile until you come to Water St.; turn left. Go under the
turnpike and over the drawbridge onto what is now Forbes
Ave. After a half dozen blocks, start up a hill which spirals
right, then left and peaks at the junction with Woodward
Ave., the first stoplight (it may not be marked). Turn right;
cross over I95 and go straight on Woodward Ave. In one and
a half miles, Woodward and the water meet at Nathan Hale
Park. Woodward Ave. turns inland here and ends as it runs
into Townsend Ave. Turn right and within a half mile you
come to Morris Cove where you'll have a fine view of New
Haven Harbor. Turn right onto Morris Cove Ave. at the end
of the cove. Turn left in half a block when it ends at Bristol
Pl. Turn right at the intersection with Lighthouse and right
again on Cove St. then left on Cora St., back to Lighthouse
Ave. and the entrance to Lighthouse Point Park. Turn right
into the park. It's a half mile to the beach proper; a lovely
beach with a bathhouse.

From the park you return to Lighthouse Rd. and within
a half mile you will find the Pardee Morris House on the
right, built in 1685 and open to the public from May 1 to

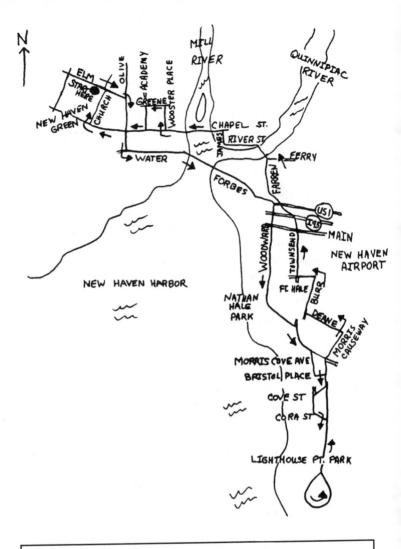

How to get there: (See the New Haven—East Rock Ride)

Nov. 1 except Saturdays. From the Morris House continue downhill to Townsend Ave. Cross Townsend onto the very short Morris Causeway to Dean St.; turn left. Continue to Burr St.; turn right and go to Fort Hale Rd., the first street on the left past the airport terminal. Turn left and ride uphill to Townsend Ave. where you turn right. Soon you will cross Main St. and I95. Go straight, past Forbes Ave. until you start downhill on Farren Ave. At the bottom of Farren, turn left onto Ferry St. Cross over the bridge, on the sidewalk, then turn left onto River St., the first street at the foot of the bridge. Go to the end of River and turn right on James. Ride one block to Chapel St. where you turn left, over the elderly Chapel St. bridge. After one and a quarter miles you'll come to Wooster Place; turn right. Make a circuit of Wooster Square Park and turn right—back onto Chapel St.—and ride the five blocks to Church St. and the Green.

17. New Haven—Sleeping Giant

Number of miles: 25
Approximate pedalling time: 3½ hours
Terrain: hilly
Surface: mostly good, some rough spots
Places to see: New Haven Green, Yale University, Sleeping
    Giant State Park, John Dickerman House, Quinnipiac
    College, Hamden

This ride starts on College St. at the Green. Go to the archway called Phelps Gate in the center of the block-long Yale University building which flanks College St. Ride through the arch and across the Old Campus to High St. Turn right and go to Grove. This is the heart of the university. Turn left on Grove and curve past the gymnasium (largest in the world, per Mr. Guinness) to the traffic light. Be careful here. Bear right past Dixwell and Goffe and turn right on Whalley Ave.

    Proceed out Whalley which bears to the right 2.4 miles from the start at the junction of Rtes. 243 and 63. Whalley is 63. In another mile you will come to the "Y" intersection of 63 and 69. Bear right onto 69. Within a half mile you'll find yourself on a two lane country road which takes you uphill past farms and a lovely lake. A mile past the lake, turn right onto Downs Rd. and skirt Lake Watrous. After the lake you have a steep uphill ride to Carmel Rd., the second road to the right after Lake Watrous, and 2.3 miles past Downs Rd. Turn right onto Carmel Rd., down to Brooks Rd. where you turn left and proceed for a mile to West Woods Rd. Turn right on West Woods. At Choate, West Woods goes right and then loops gently to the left. At Shepherd St. go left for one

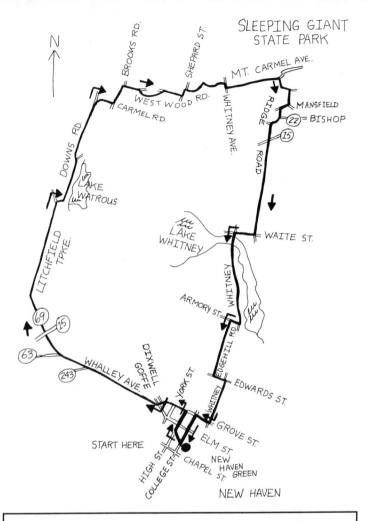

SLEEPING GIANT STATE PARK

NEW HAVEN

How to get there: take I95 to New Haven; take the Church St. ("Downtown New Haven") exit, turn right onto Church, proceed to the New Haven Green and park in the area

block and then turn right back onto West Woods, which will now take you one mile to Whitney Ave. Turn right onto Whitney then left onto Mt. Carmel Ave. On the right you will see the Jonathan Dickerman House, built in 1770. It is open on summer weekends and is worth visiting. On the left is Sleeping Giant State Park. There is a bike rack inside the entrance.

When leaving the park, proceed on Mt. Carmel past Quinnipiac College to Ridge Rd.; turn right. Ridge Rd. goes up and down for about two miles before leveling off. When you come to a "T" intersection, turn right, following Ridge Rd. as it goes up and over Rte. 22 and then bears gently to the left. Continue on Ridge Rd. for three miles to Waite St. where you turn right, run downhill to Whitney Ave. and turn left. Here is a stunning view of East Rock across Lake Whitney. You are about four miles from your starting point on the New Haven Green.

Follow Whitney Ave. to Armory St. across from the dam. Turn right, then go left on Edgehill Rd. (If you're ready for a respite, turn into Edgerton Park on the left.) Follow Edgehill (which soon changes its name to St. Ronan) to Edwards St., a "T" intersection. Turn left, go to Whitney once more and turn right. At Grove St. turn right, then turn left at College and back to your car.

18. North Lyme

Number of miles: 12½
Approximate pedalling time: 1½ hours
Terrain: definitely hilly
Surface: fair
Things to see: lovely country throughout, Eight Mile River, Hamburg, North Lyme

Mount up and turn right onto Rte. 156. Proceed uphill; at the crest you will enjoy a scene of rolling hills and pastures. After a whopping downhill, a brief uphill will deliver you to the town of Hamburg which borders the Eight Mile River. Soon after passing a Congregational church the road forks; take the left fork, Old Hamburg Rd., down to the river's edge. When the road "Ts," turn right. After turning you'll notice a good place to picnic at the riverside on your left.

When you return to Rte. 156, turn left. The road follows the Eight Mile River for a time, meandering and going up and down. Just after you cross Beaver Brook, turn right onto Beaver Brook Rd. For nearly three miles go along this two lane country road, passing farms and handsome country houses. You will pass a road coming in from the right and then arrive at the intersection of Beaver Brook, Gungy (on the left) and Grassy Hill Rds. Turn right onto Grassy Hill Rd. You pass through a beautiful forest here whose dappled light makes this a perfect ride for a summer evening. When you come out of the woods, the hill crests yielding a spacious view and a surprising field of ferns on the right. The Congregational church is set high on the hill to your left. A settled area follows this scene and there are some good downhills to the point where you turn off Grassy Hill Rd.

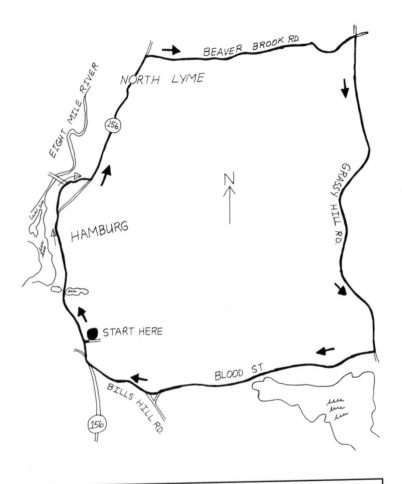

How to get there: take I95 to the Old Lyme exit, then go north on Rte. 156 toward Hamburg for about three and a half miles; turn right onto the road immediately past the sign "Nehantic State Forest 800 feet" and park

A landmark for the turn right onto Blood St. is an abandoned windmill; not of the Dutch type, it has a metal superstructure topped by narrow blades. There may not be a sign here for Blood St., so keep an eye out for the windmill. Blood St. borders Rogers Lake. This stretch is a rather densely populated resort area where there are a couple of steep hills. In about a mile and a half bear right at the fork and go right again when you "T" into Bill Hill Rd., just a few feet from the fork. Continue to the right as Bill Hill Rd. returns you to Rte. 156. Turn right when you reach 156 and in one-fifth of a mile you will be back at your starting place.

19. Old Saybrook

Number of miles: 12
Approximate pedalling time: 1¼ hours
Terrain: flat
Surface: good
Things to see: 18th century houses, Connecticut River, the
    Sound, Old Saybrook, Fenwick and the Castle Inn at
    Cornfield Point

Park at any convenient spot on Main St. Ride south on Main
(Rte. 154). In about a mile notice the store for the Hum-
phrey Pratt Tavern on the right (with the gold mortar and
pestle). At the large arrow, bear left. (Rte. 154 is now called
College St.) When you come to North Cove Rd., turn left
and follow it down to the water and around to Cromwell
Place which leads you back to College St. Turn left onto
College St. and follow it down to the riverside. There is a
marina on the right and several restaurants. A picnic lunch
can be enjoyed on the quay.

When you are ready, return to College St., turn left on
what is now Bridge St. and cross the causeway over South
Cove. This is narrow, so ride carefully. The road is now
called Maple Ave. Turn left on the other side onto Nebang
Ave. and take a mile-long circuit of Lynde Point. Back on
Maple Ave., turn left and you will soon find yourself riding
beside Long Island Sound.

In the distance, you will see what appears to be a large
stone mansion. To get to it, turn left on Hartlands Dr.,
between two stone pillars. Continue until you get to the
Castle Inn, built in 1906 to rival the grandeur of Newport.
Here you can get a room, a drink or a meal.

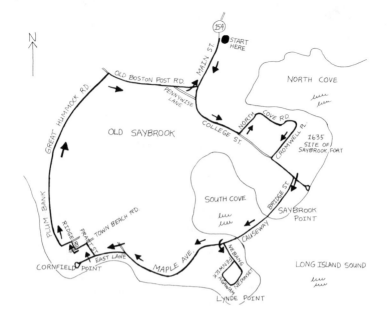

How to get there: from the north take Rte. 9 to I95, go west to Exit 67, go into Old Saybrook on Rte. 154; from the east, take I95 to Exit 67, turn left and go straight to East Main St.

When you leave the inn, turn left on Pratt Rd., left on Town Beach Rd., and immediately right on Ridge Rd. In two blocks, you'll be back on Rte. 154, now called Plum Beach Rd. It continues along the Sound, slowly swings inland, crosses Back River, and becomes Great Hammock Rd. About one and a half miles from the inn, Great Hammock Rd. "Ts" into the Old Boston Post Rd. Turn right here and return to Main St., seven-tenths of a mile away.

20. Pomfret

Number of miles: 15
Approximate pedalling time: 2 hours
Terrain: varied, some of it quite demanding
Surface: good
Things to see: Pomfret School, Annhurst College, Woodstock, Bowen Mansion, Roseland Park and Lake, Wappaquasset Pond, One Room Schoolhouse

Start the ride at the Pomfret Post Office which is located on Rt. 44 just east of the junctions of 44 and 169. Return to the junction then turn right onto Rte. 169 north. There's a real rollercoaster of a hill as you leave town. In two miles you'll pass through the campus of Annhurst College. Watch for a historical marker on the right between the college and the town of Woodstock; it designates the oldest one room schoolhouse in America which was built in 1748. It is located just off the road. At about the three mile mark, you will come to a stop sign. Turn left and continue on 169 to Woodstock. You will see a pink Victorian mansion on the left. This is the Bowen Mansion which is open to the public.

Leaving Woodstock, take a right on Child's Hill Rd. at the end of the Green and ride downhill for a fast, magnificent two mile run. At the bottom of the hill turn right onto Roseland Park Rd. In a mile you'll enter the park on your left. Roseland Park was endowed by Henry Bowen of the pink mansion in Woodstock, and it has retained its fond turn-of-the-century ambiance. The park's golf course, built in 1891, is said to be the oldest in the United States. Here you may rent a boat, swim, picnic, and play tennis. Head back to the road and turn left to resume your route.

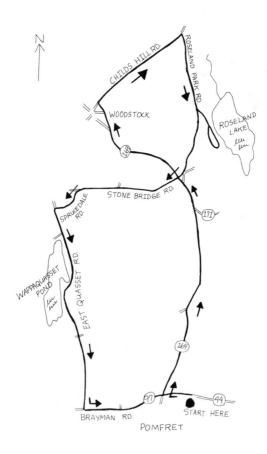

How to get there: Pomfret is a few miles west of Putnam; from the south take Rte. 52 to Exit 93 (Killingly Center), then take Rte. 101 west to Rte. 44, turn north to Pomfret; from the west take Rte. 86 to Exit 100, take Rte. 44 east to Pomfret

Turn right at Stone Bridge Rd. at the Common in South Woodstock. Cross Rte. 169. Now you face a real gear-shifter of a hill. Watch for Sprucedale Rd. on the left. Turn 45 degrees onto Sprucedale which soon "Ts" into East Quasset Rd. Turn left on East Quasset and go up a steep hill past the cemetery to the top of the ridge. Wappaquasset Pond is on your right. After passing Fox Hill Rd. there is one of the finest sights of this (or any other) ride: a winding country road, rolling meadows bounded by stone walls, cows, huge trees . . . all the ingredients of your favorite New England calendar! East Quasset Rd. "Ts" into Brayman Rd. (Rte. 97); turn left. Here you have a mighty hill to master to regain Pomfret on the ridge. Cross Rte. 169 and return to the post office.

21. Ridgefield

Number of miles: 12
Approximate pedalling time: 2 hours
Terrain: definitely hilly
Surface: good
Things to see: Ridgefield, Aldrich Museum of Contemporary
Art, Lake Mamanasco

Start in the parking lot of the Aldrich Museum which has an exciting collection of contemporary painting and sculpture. The sculpture is outdoors and free for you to enjoy. Turn right onto Main St. and proceed through the shopping area. Turn right at Prospect St. at the first caution light. When you come to East Ridge Rd. turn right and go uphill. The road soon levels off, then goes downhill to a "T" intersection with Rte. 102. Turn right to return to Main St. Turn left at Main, then right at the fountain where Rte. 35 joins Main St. Turn right again onto High Ridge Rd. Go to the junction of High Ridge and King Lane; continue on High Ridge by snaking left and immediately right. At Catoonah St. turn right and return to Main St. Turn left on Main St.

Just past the Elms Inn (which has been in continuous operation since 1799) is the site of the Battle of Ridgefield. In 1777, 600 militiamen under the command of Generals Wooster and Arnold attempted to cut off 1800 British troops. Wooster was killed and Arnold and his men finally withdrew as they were outflanked. There is a marker here inscribed:"On April 27, 1777 died 8 patriots who were laid in these grounds companioned by sixteen British soldiers, living their enemies, dying their guests."

The route for the next four miles to Lake Mamanasco is

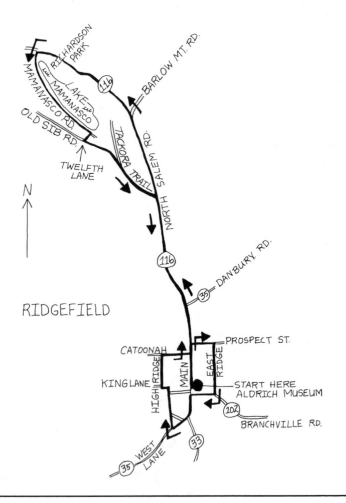

How to get there: from the east take the Merritt Parkway to Rte. 33, proceed north to Ridgefield; from the west take the Merritt Parkway to Rte. 7 and proceed north until it joins with 33, then take 33 to Ridgefield mostly downhill (but uphill on the way back). When you come to a "Y" intersection bear left on Rte. 116. Watch for the entrance to Richardson Park on the left. This wooded property is open to the public for hiking and picnicking. Turn left onto Mamanasco Rd. You are about seven miles into the ride here. This route skirts the lake. About halfway around is Peatt's Fishing Camp where there is a beach and a tiny short order restaurant. At Peatt's you may swim or rent a boat. Turn right at Twelfth Lane at the end of the lake. You'll have to push up this one. At the top of the hill turn left on Old Sib Rd., which soon joins Tackora Trail. Bear right on Rte. 116 at the junction and head back to Ridgefield and the Aldrich Museum lot.

22. Rowayton

Number of miles: 8½
Approximate pedalling time: 1 hour
Terrain: one gradual hill and one very steep climb, otherwise flat
Surface: fair
Things to see: Tokeneke (Darien), Wilson Cove, the Sound, village of Rowayton, Three Mile River

From the parking lot, turn left on Old Farm Rd. The area of Tokeneke is dotted with huge houses and equally extravagant NO TRESPASSING signs, but the public roads provide a sufficient glimpse of manorial life. Turn left on Searles Rd., and right on Five Mile River Rd. which reveals a view of the little village of Rowayton on the other side of the river (which is jammed with yachts). Five Mile River Rd. dead-ends at a turnaround bordered by a stone wall. Turn around and head back up the road. When it "Ts" with Tokeneke Rd. turn right and cross the bridge into Rowayton. Here the name of the road changes to Cudlipp. At the first light take a sharp left onto Rowayton Ave. Go gradually uphill several blocks. Turn right on Devil's Garden Rd. You'll go steeply uphill now until Devil's Garden "Ts" into Highland Ave.; turn right. At the second stop sign turn left onto Wilson Ave. and go half a block to Bluff Ave.

Turn right on Bluff. You'll enjoy the downhill ride back to sea level where there is a treat in store: you cross over a small bridge at Wilson Cove and from this vantage you can see Bell and Tavern Islands and Wilson Point. Continue straight on Bluff which now changes its name to Westmere Ave. At the first stop sign turn right on Yarmouth Rd. and

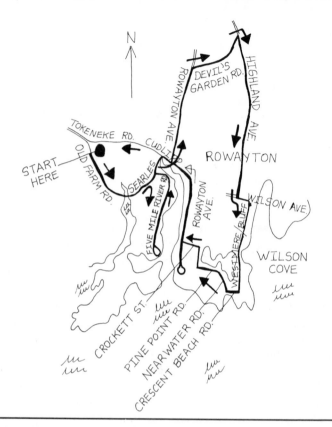

How to get there: from the west take I95 to Exit 12, turn right at the foot of the ramp, cross Locust Hill Rd. and turn right in about half a block into the parking lot of the Tokeneke School where you may park; from the east take I95 to Exit 11, turn right at the bottom of the ramp and go to Rte. 136 (before the RR underpass), and turn right onto 136 (Tokeneke Rd.); continue on it until you come to Old Farm Rd. on the right; turn right, cross Locust Hill Rd. and pull into the parking lot behind the school

then immediately right at the next stop sign onto Crescent Beach Rd. This is a lovely private beach. Head inland by following the road as it curves right, becoming Ensign Rd., then turn left at the first street, then right again and left at the "T" with Nearwater. Shortly you will see a stunning contemporary house perched above the salt marsh like a Cubist stork. About a block from this striking structure, turn left onto Crockett St. which will take you over to Rowayton Ave., the village's main thoroughfare.

Turn left so you can explore the eastern end of Rowayton Ave. and the boat yards, then turn around and enjoy the flavor of the village as you pass its appealing yards, yacht brokerages, shops, and restaurants. Stay on Rowayton Ave. until you come to the light marking the intersection with Cudlipp St.; bear left, go over the bridge into Darien, and return to Old Farm Rd. and the Tokeneke School.

23. Salisbury—Falls Village

Number of miles: 17
Approximate pedalling time: 2½ hours
Terrain: varied, some tough hills, some rolling country, some flat stretches
Surface: generally good
Things to see: Salisbury and Falls Village, Lime Rock Park, Berkshire foothills, Salmon Creek Valley

Park at the White Hart Inn on Main St. Head north on Rte. 44 east. In a half mile you'll go up Mt. Wetauwanchu and crest at the entrance to Salisbury School. Parts of the climb are imposing but it is followed by a mile-long downhill with a view of the Berkshires. Half a mile from the bottom you'll cross the Housatonic. Take a right on Rte. 126 heading for Falls Village. This is rolling dairy country. Go over the railroad tracks and the Hollenbeck River. This stretch of river is owned by us: Property of State of Connecticut. Stop at this remarkable spot for your picnic and a swim in the swimming hole.

When 126 turns left continue straight, downhill then uphill to your left. Turn left onto Main St. On a plaque on the Green you'll learn that Housatonic means "place beyond the mountains." In Falls Village note the stately National Iron Bank. When Main St. rejoins Rte. 126, take 126 to Rte. 7. Turn right on Rte. 7 for Lime Rock three miles away. When you come to the junction with Rte. 112, go right on 112 to Lime Rock which boasts that it is "the Road Racing Center of the East."

Take the first right, Old Furnace Rd., after crossing Salmon Creek and its little falls. After an abrupt uphill the

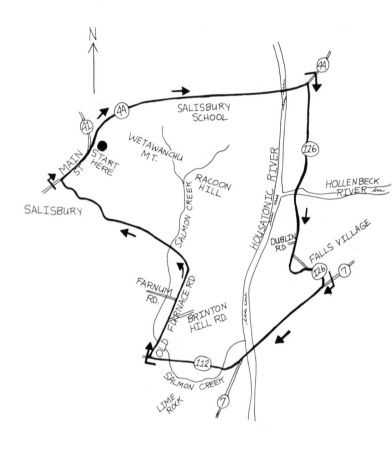

How to get there: from the southwest take Rte. 7 to Cornwall Bridge then follow Rtes. 4, 41, and 44 to Salisbury; from Hartford and the east take Rte. 44 to Salisbury

road lets you down into Salmon Creek Valley. In about a half mile, the road forks; bear left. You'll pass handsome Salmon Kill Farm (did you know that "kill" means creek?). The road follows the contours of the mountains, the tallest of which, Raccoon Hill (1100 ft.), is ahead and to your right. About a half mile past the Farnam Rd. junction the road will turn sharply left crossing the valley floor. For the next mile and a half you'll wind through lovely country on the west side of the valley before you "T" into Salisbury's Main St. Turn right. At the corner of Washinee St. enjoy the delicious spring water of the public fountain. Continue up Main St. to the White Hart.

24. Shelton—Lake Zoar

Number of miles: 22
Approximate pedalling time: 3 hours
Terrain: very demanding on the west side of the river, easy riding on the east side
Surface: good on 110 and 34, only fair on 111
Things to see: the Housatonic River Valley, Derby and Shelton, Lake Zoar, Stevenson Dam, Monroe, Indian Well State Park

Enter Indian Well State Park and park at the first available spot (to avoid an unnecessary climb back up to Rte. 110 to start the ride). Plan to go for a swim here in the placid Housatonic after your ride. Turn right onto 110. The first third of this ride is very demanding. There are several long inclines, including a one-miler at the start of the ride. Proceed west on 110 through sparsely settled country to Rte. 111, about six miles from the start of your ride.

Turn right on 111. This is a secondary road, the surface is irregular and the shoulders aren't clearly marked. In half a mile you'll come to the Township of Monroe. Its tiny Green has massive trees and is flanked by traditional houses and churches. In this vicinity Rochambeau's army encamped en route to Yorktown and that fateful encounter. In another four miles, the road to the hamlet of Stevenson comes in on your right. Turn onto it and ride the block down to the post office and general store. Watch for the huge bump in the road just before rejoining Rte. 111. Turn right on 111, go under the railroad tracks and then turn right onto Rte. 34. You are now about a half mile from the Stevenson Dam. The Crossroads Drive-In is on the right just

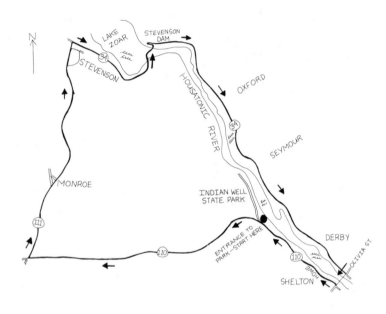

How to get there: from the west take the Merritt Parkway to Exit 52 (Rte. 8), turn north on Rte. 8, get off at Exit 14, follow signs to Shelton on Rte. 110 to Indian Well State Park, two miles north of Shelton. From the east take Rte. 34 to Shelton, turn right after crossing the bridge (110) and proceed north to the park

after you turn onto 34. Just before crossing the dam you'll spot Zoar Beach which is open to the public for a fee. Cross the dam, then ride south to Oxford, Seymour and Derby. When you enter Derby notice the Hull Dye and Print Works on the right; it is typical of the industries which dot the Valley. (The canal between the road and the factory provides water for cooling the machinery.) At the corner of Rte. 34 (Roosevelt Drive) and Olivia St. turn right and cross the Housatonic into the town of Shelton. Turn right onto Howe Ave. (Rte. 110) and ride north to Indian Well State Park.

25. Southbury—Woodbury

Number of miles: 14½
Approximate pedalling time: 2 hours
Terrain: generally flat, three moderate hills
Surface: good but some poor spots and narrow shoulders
Things to see: Woodbury and Southbury, lovely countryside,
the Curtis House

Park your car just off Rte. 6 at the intersection of Rtes. 6 and 67, as you enter Southbury. Head north on Rte. 6 east and 67 north. Turn left onto 67 west when it leaves Rte. 6. Just before crossing the bridge at the bottom of the hill you will see a dirt road on the right which leads to the riverbank and a fine spot for picnicking. Two miles from your turn onto 67, mostly uphill, you will come to the junction with Rte. 172. Turn right onto 172, also called Transylvania Rd.—shades of Dracula! The junction is also called Pine Corners. The surface of this road is typical of your Transylvanian roads—not so good. The road forks almost immediately; bear right. Soon the road goes abruptly left and downhill. You pass Woodlake and Bear Hill Rd. and, in about one quarter mile you will come to a "T" intersection. This is Rte. 317, although it may not be marked. Turn left and shortly thereafter turn right onto West Side Rd. Soon you will come to a "Y" where the left branch goes abruptly uphill and is called Lighthouse Hill Rd. Bear right, staying on West Side Rd. which curves downhill. Turn left onto Westwood Rd. which comes in from the left. Then turn right onto Jack's Bridge Rd. Jack's little bridge spans the Weekeepeemee River. The right bank of the river is accessible and fine for picnicking. Jack's Bridge Rd. "Ts" with Rte. 47. Turn right and take 47

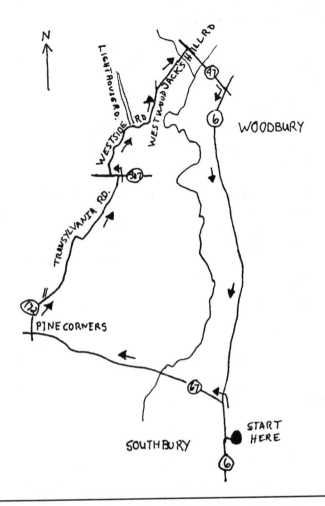

N

LIGHTHOUSE RD.

WESTSIDE RD.

WESTWOOD

JACKS HILL RD.

47

6

WOODBURY

307

TRANSYLVANIA RD.

12

PINE CORNERS

67

SOUTHBURY

START HERE

6

How to get there: from the south take Rte. 63 to 67,
then 67 west to Southbury, or Rte. 8 or 84 north to their
respective intersections with 67 west; from the north
take 67 or 6 to Southbury

into Woodbury. At the intersection of 47 with Rte. 6 turn right onto Rte. 6. This is a well-travelled road but there is a shoulder and an ample sidewalk. If you have pannier bags on your bike and cash in your pocket you might enjoy visiting some of Woodbury's numerous antique shops for some treasures. Soon you'll pass the Curtis House, Connecticut's oldest inn, which has been in business since 1754. Return to Southbury by continuing on Rte. 6.

26. Storrs

Number of miles: 12
Approximate pedalling time: 1½ hours
Terrain: definitely hilly
Surface: good
Things to see: the University of Connecticut, an old stone
  mill, tumbling streams, and lovely countryside
  throughout

Start at the intersection of Dog Lane and Rte. 195, just
before (or past) the main part of the University of Connecticut. Park behind the Universal Food Store. Mount up and
turn left on Dog Lane. Go downhill about three-fourths of a
mile to where Dog Lane "Ts" into Bundy Lane; turn right.
In a little less than a mile, at the stop sign, continue straight
on Farrell Rd. After about a half mile you will come to the
fork of Hanks Hill Rd. and Stone Hill Rd. Bear right, staying
on Hanks Hill. Just past the fork, at the mill pond, there is a
sign that states, "Here on Hanks Hill in 1810 the first silk
mill in America was built by Rodney Hanks." The mill itself
is not here because it was removed lock, stone, and board by
Henry Ford for his Dearborn Museum.

  In another half mile you turn right. There's no road sign
but it is East Rd. It's a very steep uphill but there is a grand
view at the crest where you can take a rest before turning
left onto Rte. 195 where you soon start a mile-long downhill
run. As you tear along look over to your left and you will see
a stunning view of the hills. At the bottom of the hill you
continue on the flat for another mile until you come to the
intersection of Rte. 195 and Chaffeeville Rd. Turn left onto
Chaffeeville which meanders for three miles through the

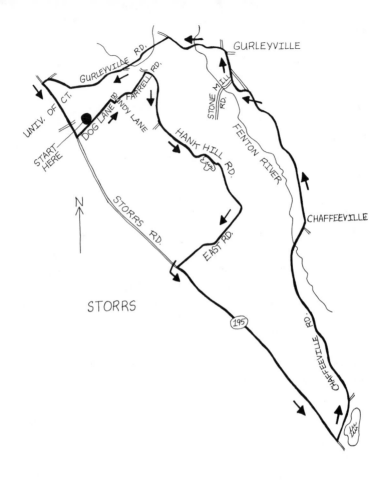

How to get there: from the northwest, take Rte. 86 to Exit 99, bear south on Rte. 195 to Storrs; from the southwest, take I91 to Exit 67 (Middletown), take Rte. 66 and Rte. 6 to 195, turn north to Storrs

countryside and then curves alongside a little river. Look for a sign, "Gurleyville Grist Mill," on the left side and a road going steeply down to the river (Stonemill Rd.). Take it and you will come upon a serene scene: a narrow stretch of bottom land, a small cheerful river and an old stone mill. This is the spot for a picnic! When you are ready, rejoin Chaffeeville Rd. and continue on to the next intersection where Chaffeeville, Gurleyville and Codfish Falls roads meet. Turn left onto Gurleyville. After a short stretch the road starts steeply uphill but soon levels off and then snakes around an enormous meadow as it returns to Rte. 195 in the middle of UCONN's campus. Here you can make a tour of the campus, or you can turn left onto 195 and ride about a half mile back to your starting place.

27. Stratford—Lordship

Number of miles: 12½
Approximate pedalling time: 1½ hours
Terrain: flat
Surface: mostly good, some poor paving
Things to see: Judson House Museum, American Shakespeare
Festival Theater, Bridgeport Airport, Long Island Sound
at Lordship

Park on West Broad St. and turn right. At Academy Hill Rd.
turn left. On your right halfway up the brief hill stands the
Judson House Museum (1723) which is open on Wednes-
days, Saturdays and Sundays from 11:00 A.M. to 5:00 P.M.
There is a small fee. At the top of Academy Hill turn right
onto Elm St. When you come to the entrance of the American Shakespeare Festival Theater, turn into the grounds.
You may picnic on the lawn. On leaving the theater turn
left on Elm St. In a few blocks turn left again and ride down
to the launching area to watch the boats. Return to Elm St.
and turn left. Elm "Ts" into Main; turn left. You are now on
Stratford Point. After passing the airport you'll come to a
"Y"; take the left fork which is Short Beach Rd. At Lighthouse Avenue turn right. Lighthouse "Ts" into Prospect
Drive. Turn left here and proceed to the lighthouse, then
turn around and ride back down Prospect to Cove Place on
your left. Turn left onto Cove and ride a short stretch to the
Sound, where you will turn right onto Park Blvd.

Park Blvd. ends when it "Ts" into Lordship Rd. Turn
right and immediately left on Ocean Ave. Then turn left
again on Washington Parkway. Washington Parkway "Ts"
into Beach Drive; go left. There is a sea wall here bounded

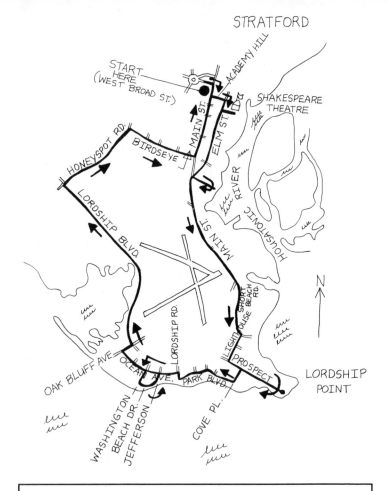

How to get there: from the east and west, take I95 to Exit 32 at Stratford and go to West Broad St.; from the north take Rte. 8 to 108, go south on 108 to US1, cross US1 and bear right on North Parade St., turn right on Main St., go under the turnpike and go to West Broad St.

by giant rocks to climb over, fish from and sit on, and there are a couple of restaurants facing the water. (In this sober little community only beer and cider may be served.) After your R and R at the water's edge, continue on Beach Drive heading east. Turn left on Ocean Ave. and proceed until it "Ts" into Oak Bluff Ave. Turn right. When Oak Bluff intersects with Lordship turn left. You will now cross a great meadow. Ride past the airport. Just beyond the entrance, Lordship Blvd. merges with Access Rd. At the junction of Lordship with Honeyspot Rd. turn right. Proceed to Birdseye Rd. Turn right. When Birdseye meets Main St. go left. In a few blocks you will see West Broad St. and your car.

28. Waterford—New London

Number of miles: 13¾
Approximate pedalling time: 1¾ hours
Terrain: mostly flat, a couple of steep hills
Surface: only fair in Waterford, good in New London
Things to see: Atlantic Ocean, Thames River and New
London Harbor, Harkness Memorial State Park, Ocean
Beach Park

Start the ride at the Waterford High School parking lot just east of the junction of US1 and Rte. 156, on the left side. Proceed west on 156 about a half mile to Great Neck Rd. (Rte. 213), where you turn left. Great Neck narrows so use the sidewalk on this stretch. Just before Great Neck swings to the left, down toward the Harkness Estate, you'll catch a stunning glimpse of the ocean. About 3.5 miles into the ride, you reach the entrance to Harkness Memorial State Park. We recommend you stop here to visit the Newport-style mansion with its enormous lawns and beautiful gardens.

Return to Rte. 213 and turn right following signs to New London. At the first stop sign, turn right. At the next stop sign turn left. (The O'Neill Theater is on the right.) Turn right when the road "Ts" into Niles Hill Rd. Go up Niles Hill. At the traffic light turn right onto Ocean Ave., following the signs to Ocean Beach Park. Ocean Ave. is broad but very busy in the summer. When you reach Neptune Ave., turn right and ride to the entrance to Ocean Beach Park. The park has a wide beach, well maintained boardwalk, rides, restaurants, an arcade, miniature golf and a water slide. There is an admission fee.

Return to Neptune Ave., cross Ocean Ave. and turn left

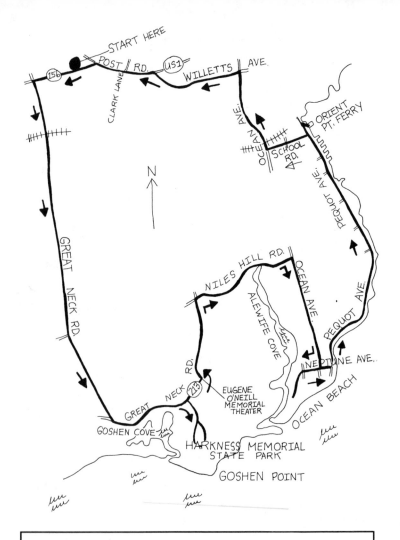

How to get there: from the east or west take I95 to Exit 75, then go east on US1 to the junction of Rte. 156 west; turn right at the junction, onto Rte. 156

onto Pequot. (Pequot is Mott Ave. to the right.) You will enjoy an unobstructed view of New London's outer harbor as you ride along Pequot. As you approach downtown New London, you'll enter an area featuring small marinas and restaurants.

At School St., turn left and climb back up to Ocean Ave.; turn right. In less than a mile, you'll come to Willetts Ave. Turn left up a gentle incline, then downhill to US1. There is a stop sign at the junction of Willetts and US1. Make your left hand turn carefully onto this busy highway. At the next traffic light, at Clark Lane, be alert again. Go straight ahead, getting into the left lane so that you can turn 45 degrees to the left onto Rte. 156 west, and return to the parking lot just beyond the intersection.

29. West Cornwall

Number of miles: 11
Approximate pedalling time: 1½ hours
Terrain: rolling on the west side of the Housatonic,
    hilly on the east
Surface: good
Things to see: an authentic covered bridge, the Housatonic
    River and Housatonic Meadows State Park, Furnace
    Creek, the Deck Restaurant

Park anywhere on West Cornwall's hilly main street. You should explore this tiny village, perched on the side of the restless, beautiful Housatonic River, either before or after your ride. There are interesting shops, including the Tollhouse. The Deck Restaurant and Gift Shop serves good food—indoors and out. In clear weather you can dine on the deck itself which is built out over a rocky brook and waterfall. A stop here is a great reward, especially after your ride. Another plus on this ride is that there are numerous lovely places to picnic, either on the banks of the Housatonic or along Furnace Creek.

Start the ride by crossing the river over the covered bridge. Turn left on the other side and go south on Rte. 7 along the river's edge. You may see canoeists or swimmers going tubing here where the river is frolicsome but not overly dangerous. You will see very few houses on the ride as your road dips and winds gently up and down hill and through the woods. In two and a half miles you will come to a campsite which is one of the most inviting we've seen: Housatonic Meadows Campground. One mile further along brings you to the park's adjoining picnic grounds for non-

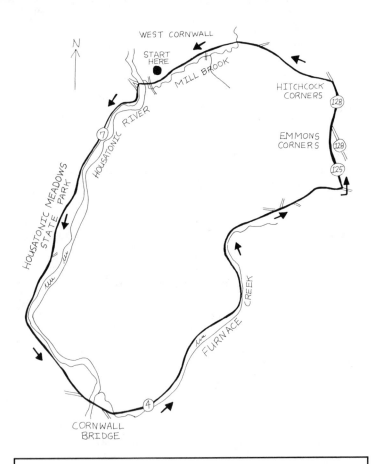

How to get there: West Cornwall is in the northwest corner of Connecticut. From Torrington take Rte. 4 west. At the junction of Rte. 4 with Rte. 43 and Rte. 128, take Rte. 128 north into West Cornwall; from the south take Rte. 202 north to New Preston; from there take Rte. 45 to Rte. 7 which will take you into West Cornwall

campers. In about four miles you will come to the junction where Rte. 4 joins Rte. 7. Bear left and cross the river at the Cornwall Bridge. Stop on the bridge for a while to take in the scene: river, rocks, clouds above, shades of green, houses tucked into hills. There is a fork just over the river. Bear left on Rte. 4 where you must master a steep hill. Rte. 4 borders Furnace Creek and there are many great picnic sites just off the road. We stopped and had lunch about a half mile from the fork. A lovely spot with the creek right under our feet. About eight miles into the ride you will come to the junction of Rte. 4 and Rte. 125; turn left and go up a steep hill toward West Cornwall through woods and forest. Soon Rte. 128 joins 125 at an oblique angle to the right. About a half mile from town you will start a long winding descent into the village—a great way to end the ride!

30. Wethersfield

Number of miles: 11½
Approximate pedalling time: 1½ hours
Terrain: varied, some steep hills
Surface: generally good, some poor spots
Things to see: Buttolph-Williams House, Silas Deane House,
    Joseph Webb House, Issac Stevens House, Old Academy
    Museum, Comstock-Ferre Co., Wethersfield Cove,
    Millwoods Park

Start this ride on Main St. across from the Comstock-Ferre
Co., Connecticut's oldest seed company and a good place to
browse. Ride north on Main St. past many handsome houses
to the shore of Wethersfield Cove and Common. This is a
busy boating scene in the summer. Return down Main St.
and turn left on Marsh St. Ride past the cemetery and turn
right on Broad St. The marvelous Buttolph-Williams House
(1692) stands silently on the corner. This house contains an
excellent collection of period pieces including an extensive-
ly furnished kitchen. Proceed on Broad St. to the Wethersfield Green. Bear left and ride down the left side of the
Green. At the end turn right and come back up the right
side as far as Garden St. Turn left on Garden and go to Main.
Turn right. Pass the Old Academy Museum. In another
block you will come to a trio of stately houses. The Silas
Deane House (1766) is the first of these. General Washington planned the capture of Fort Ticonderoga in this elegant
house. The Joseph Webb House (1752) was also graced by
the presence of General Washington for here he met with
Rochambeau in 1781 to plan the last campaigns of the
Revolution. The Issac Stevens House (1788), while more

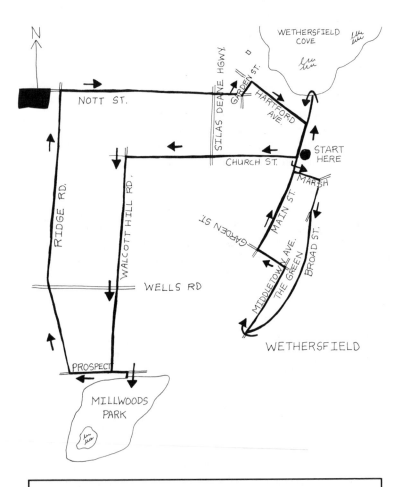

How to get there: from the north and south take I91 to Exit 26; if coming from the north, you will exit onto Marsh St., follow it to Main St.; if coming from the south you will exit onto Great Meadow Rd., turn left again on Marsh St. and go to Main St.

modest, has an interesing collection of children's clothes and paraphernalia. Don't neglect to take note of the 19th century elegance of the Capt. Hurbert House across the street from the Stevens House.

Now proceed to the intersection with Church St. and turn left. Go uphill. Cross the Silas Deane Highway. Go uphill again to Walcott Hill Rd.; turn left. At the crest of the hill cross Wells Rd. and go downhill to Prospect St. Turn left at Prospect and then right into Millwoods Park. Here you may swim and picnic. There is a beach and dressing rooms. After visiting Millwoods Park, turn left onto Prospect St., ride uphill to Ridge Rd. and turn right. The road crests at Wells St. You will start downhill after crossing Rutledge. Turn right on Nott St. where, after a brief uphill spurt, you get a nice downhill run. Cross the Silas Deane Highway again, go to Garden St. and turn left. Cross Hartford Ave. and go in the entrance driveway to the Solomon Wells House (1774). Enjoy the expanse of lawn down to the cove, then turn left on Hartford Ave. which will lead you to Main St. and your car.